Sighted Stones

poems by

Sarah Mead Wyman

Finishing Line Press
Georgetown, Kentucky

Sighted Stones

Copyright © 2018 by Sarah Mead Wyman
ISBN 978-1-63534-560-5 First Edition
All rights reserved under International and Pan-American Copyright Conventions. No part of this book may be reproduced in any manner whatsoever without written permission from the publisher, except in the case of brief quotations embodied in critical articles and reviews.

ACKNOWLEDGMENTS

"Basket," *AMP*
"Braque's Athena" was a finalist in the 2017 Stephen A. DiBiase Poetry Contest.
"Braque's Measurements," "Bull Wall: American Royale, Robert Morris,"
"Urbana #6, Richard Diebenkorn," and "Fur Skirt," *Home Planet News*
"Bucket: Democracy / Theocracy, Jonathan Wahl" *Reading Objects*
 "Enlightening Jack;" "Popinjay in the Japonica." *Shawangunk Review*
 "Fishbone;" "Wet Exit." *Petrichor Review*
"Lumina 1," "Lumina 7," "Lumina 22," *Lumina*
"Message" *Mudfish*
"Monterey Bay;" "Popinjay in the Japonica." *Shawangunk Review*
"Popinjay in the Japonica." *Riverine: An Anthology of Hudson Valley Writers.*
"Ritual" *Chronogram*
"Untitled (Yellow Collage), Richard Diebenkorn," *Ekphrasis*
 "Walls & Flowers." *1995/1996 Anthology of Magazine Verse & Yearbook of American Poetry.*
"Walls & Flowers." *Quarry*
"Wet Exit." *A Slant of Light: Contemporary Women Writers of the Hudson Valley.*

With gratitude to William R. Harmon and his rendered rabbits.

Publisher: Leah Maines
Editor: Christen Kincaid
Cover Art: "Sojourn" (2015) by Lydia Cleaveland, Clio Miller, Ann Wyman, Sarah Wyman. Photo credit: Sarah Wyman
Author Photo: Delphi Cleaveland
Cover Design: Elizabeth Maines McCleavy

Printed in the USA on acid-free paper.
Order online: www.finishinglinepress.com

Author inquiries and mail orders:
Finishing Line Press
P. O. Box 1626
Georgetown, Kentucky 40324
U. S. A.

Table of Contents

Message 1
Untitled (Yellow Collage), Richard Diebenkorn 2
Arshile Gorky 3
Athena, Georges Braque 4
Braque's Measurements 5
Bull Wall: American Royale, Robert Morris 6
Molting Exoskeletons, Robert Morris 7
Urbana #6, Richard Diebenkorn 8
Coffee, Richard Diebenkorn 9
Lumina 1, Jamie Bennett 10
Lumina 7, Jamie Bennett 11
Lumina 22, Jamie Bennet 12
Bucket: Democracy / Theocracy, Jonathan Wahl 13
Basket 14
Spider 15
Blue Dandy 16
Popinjay in the Japonica 17
Monterey Bay 19
Repo Man 20
Ritual 21
Louisiana Mudline 22
Wet Exit 23
Fishbone 24
Squaring the Circling Way 25
Walls & Flowers 26
Fur Skirt 27
Frog Season 28
Enlightening Jack 30
Times Square Bracelet 31
Fox 32

Message

When I opened your letter
I was eating a pomegranate.
Really, I was
with the startling red juice
splayed on the cutting board.

I had to get up
in the middle of reading
wander around
talk to a friend.

What was inside was
too big for an envelope
too much for the stamps
in the corner.

So full of seeds
and seeping with blood
I couldn't take more, being already
as full as the moon.

Untitled (Yellow Collage), Richard Diebenkorn

It seemed she would stay forever
folded like a yellow sun
upon its chair.
Even the elbows echoed each other
as her hair tumbled out of view.
Still, we believed her locks there,
brown behind her back.

Woman who went
like the watery blue
streaked along her skirt sections
and a bracelet that banded
the arm by her chin:
tiny rivulet of departure.

Only paper, after all
she could have melted
under a spilled drink.
A touch of flame
would have burst her to ashes.

Heavy in their paint
the edges warped
where they followed her form,
sought air so she seemed to lean
forward, unhooked from her moorings
however solid in that seat
smelling of studio,
womanly and fine.

One day she stood up,
uncrossed her limbs
so the legs could walk
her body from the room
so her arm could raise
and wave goodbye.

Arshile Gorky

By taking up a hero's name
the Armenian cast himself
as a Greek warrior whose spoils,
thrown in a corner,
mounted jewels to the rafters,
whose curls were crowned
in gilt laurel leaves. And yet,
this painter captured not
another nation's slaves, but merely
the swoops and darts of insects,
the surreal trajectory of a humming bird
as rhythms of the natural world
recapitulate in paint
when eye is keen
and brush knows how to follow.
So watery reds merged violet blues
seeped sepia, not blood
when lines were crossed
where the liquid tint allowed its drips
as the artist lay low
to *look into grass*
a hot Virginia summer.
He followed an ant up its blade
to sharpen his eye
on the rough underside of a green shoot
only to hang, at last, his body
there in the cool studio,
an arrow in the heel
too soon,
violent sting of the chiseled head
severing the tendon rope, cutting
the body down to dark earth.

Athena, Georges Braque

The horses rear in unison
as the straps stay lax
and their feminine underbellies
pull them into panels of light
so their darker charge,
standing in the chariot,
must keep her knees beneath
her, tied in by biomorphic arabesques
of nothingness but the wind behind,
captured in a bubble that echoes
fluttering shoulder blades
like wings or slackening sails
below a helmet softened to a stocking cap
she wishes she could swap
for equine mane and be the one
to lead the pair faster
free of the wheel and snowy white
stuck in the spokes like ice.
Through the curved shadow
that shields her,
poor excuse for an ironed chiton,
the long lozenge of a fading form
wants to ride her bareback
and bear her back to Athens.

Braque's Measurements

Thin fish, an oily layer of paint
on canvas laid upon a dish.
Thick outline in same gray
that drew the plate itself
still downward sliding
by a blue pitcher left out to dry
as *units of tactile measurement:*
foot, arm's length, hand's breadth
hold the memory of the body
that crafted it, identical
span between fingers,
knuckled segments to scale
the reach into a dimension
where fish float, where fork and moon
perfectly match as silver flattens
into ornament not instrument
of illumination or ingestion,
just a well-tined plunge
through darkness
to the shaved side of a mullet
beached upon a tray.
The carafe's ready to fill the cups
and your eyes across the varnish
fathom the depths below
a table that holds all in place.

Bull Wall: American Royale, Robert Morris

Have you seen this wall,
steel cut in Kansas City
where bulls stampede
their empty shadows
through two thicknesses
of corten welded at the x?

The ones in front
break with hooves,
ready to gore their two-pronged
crowns if their might
doesn't tumble them headlong
to somersaults spearing earth flesh
instead of us.

And others pause to look on,
lesser kings in cowboy land
still muscled enough to do the job.
Like us, they are filled with the fury
of our shadowed history,
horned royalty brought to the prairies
and caught in the factory's metal mural
where the charge goes on.

Molting Exoskeletons, Robert Morris

What is a resin-soaked shroud to do?
Lumbering over a wooden manikin,
setting its linen down to listen,
the hardened fabric
finds its shape as the grounded pull
tugs it earthward,
as the slick face and long arm
allow a wet touch that does not stay.
No stick to the surface
but a hollow remembrance
of contact, shades of some soul
or object of ridicule
now cornered as the fool.
Golden shells, animate in amber
honey up in a frozen
crust of time that captures
each one of us
and lets us go—

Urbana # 6, Richard Diebenkorn

On Diebenkorn's black carpet,
legless shoes trot past
a waterfall that soaks
the shag with its second cascade
dropping underground, and contours
of the sandy scape create
a desert-wise attempt to tie up
loose odds and ends
while a ship sails by without an ocean
and a purple sock
could be a cat's tail flickering.
Hardly a spot to sit and rest
as the yellow burns its square head through
the floor despite red spatters
that cry quietly for help.
Meager attempts to tidy up
the tiled room corner
end in a tilted broom
handle and a dash off to the right:
the green canoe cast out to sea.

Coffee, Richard Diebenkorn

By an open window, she clutches her coffee
in hands that match the hue of long legs
as though all were of a piece this morning,
the way wind tumbles through openings,
a sea in the near distance sending its salt
to her hair, blued like a cap on her skull
that might tilt and tuck itself into the teacup,
a sip that could suck her form away from this scene
tunneling down through the porcelain,
taking her round-backed wicker chair with her,
all imploding over the fragile edge, rolled like a canvas
stuffed neatly and leaving only the emerald carpet behind.

Lumina 1, Jamie Bennett

I wanted to say, look - the sun's shaft
returning, but now the reflected frame
squares my view in a panoramic shot
that casts light where blood dries
on a plate and the round lens translates
to oblong so all corners are lost to the test.

They tried to smooth your tracks with a hoe,
hose down the menace that rises from the golden pit
with a child's spiral route that presses
back darkness, each step flat as a sneaker,
soft sunk with glancing
weight, and one lace left behind
sews shut the twisted path.

The gleam of gold melts like inedible chocolate
to bond medallions invested in calm
to weigh the captured light on retinas circled in precious metal
as though one could secure the chevroned wish
lying like a heart,
as though darkened warmth could hold our hooped path
aloft, as though the sun could punch
its way back to roundness and lift the sable calm
out of its own depth to temper the crisp glare of day.

Lumina 7, Jamie Bennett

Flowers have hollowed out their nests of stone,
inverted birds who fly deeper than earth clouds.
Brown dirt gives way to loamy rivulets that tie the planet's
many faces in a thread network skeleton.

The sunken blooms defy the expected float
and only remnant pedestrians remind the creek
that they have left their element,
watering fresh, walking the resistant
planks of twigs as though disks were hitched
and nails could hold.

Someone returned to sew each pistiled eye in place
so the bouquet stays, raising its amber anthers
while doomed dahlias blossom a crowded cry
above the peep hole where snow creeps warmth away
and red wefts across the dry fall field.

Lumina 22, Jamie Bennett

If I could sew this weird cleavage
shut where even the Singer
balks and spins her wavy retreat
port side to a flipped ship
and each nipple of calm
attempts to stir the wake,
then you could belt the parting hands
like splitting boards
that grasp for the bolted clench.

Song sung by a dreamy maggot
imagining the buzz, opposite a bleach spot
that glows in the light left on
after they swept the parquet clean
of ashy mites that pause in air then fall.

But no lipstick crush coming from behind
would settle for such scaffolded reproach,
separation stapled into documents
that bear the dazzled sear
of an iron left too long
beside a stain that stays despite
all laddered intention to raise the eyes.

Bucket: Democracy / Theocracy, Jonathan Wahl

His words fell as punctured stars
seeped into the bucket
of what he wished to say.
He could talk his way
out of any cupped hand,
water through the fingers,
a breach of support
hanging by a thread.
But this was different.
Making his way
to the tin circle could have been his triumph.
Instead, he let the juice run out
as roundness ripened to a trickle.
Factions patterned their pin holes
where light shadowed
the arena of use
on a rounded floor.

Then, through the broken bullhorn, heavy in its emptiness, he spoke: Fill this gunmetal vessel with snow; illuminate the jealous lampshade. No snuffed candle here, but a blind reflection in the dingy tin of a skirt over the head, inverted petticoat revolution, hot to the touch, where a singed handle marks the passage past relief of water. An indifferent sacrum bleeding stars drips democracy, sharp lights of leakage on a nation longing for a sip. Slanted cell walls open to the sky, too slick to climb, too finely fused to shape the eternal circle. That fight-heightening splash in the face, split rope holding back where swings a chunk of metal tree, a chiseled orb, truncated arrow, lopped spear, makes merely a blunt threat aimed at the thirsty earth. No ammo.

Basket

The spray of deep greens
has reseeded itself
and grown again amidst
waxy succulents that expanded
all summer, pushing
their pale gray stars
across the basket you planted
and roped in with a now-rusting
chain, like the one you wore
long around your neck
the day you told me
what you carried,
held underground for now.

And along with the green shoots
surprising, a note on my door
saying you'd been there,
tacking your presence
boldly to my board,
a bright flash in the day,
a leaf turned to catch sun
when I'd wondered
what had become of you
and how you might carry on,
leaving your sheets behind,
sowing words along your path.

Spider

The strength of a spider leg
lifted athletically at the shoulder
or is it hip?
traverses the surface of your book
with a light touch that elevates
her whole body, as though she wished
to finger many times over
the pages left to read.
Why shouldn't her tiny mind
eviscerate the volume?
Let her capture
its images in a full-body massage
of crispy paper, inked oil of thought.

Best to let the eager spider
finish your studies for you.
Best to turn your mighty body
to me, tickling your limbs upon
my open binding, your threat
of itchy bite upon my neck
stretched out like a web
to capture, to wrap my words
about you and spin the covers shut.

Blue Dandy

Green velvet
jacket over pin stripes
in blue. Blue rush azul
round each ankle,
and the dandy fashions
a new look
down the sidewalk.
Flanneur whose waltz
over cobblestones
makes the men look
past their papers,
makes one wish
he could
dance the bluestone
to dust.

Popinjay in the Japonica

Dame Elaine shined silver, wore lace, and painted teacups.
Some decades past, wrapped in cream satin, with orange
blossoms in her hand, she'd made a match with a Rock-
erfeller, his family mansion, and vast grounds.
I, the gardener, enter the picture, a fly
on the wall, tending the boxwood, pruning this tree

or that. My quiet life on the estate, country
calm after city living, pleases me. A cou-
ple of marriages taxied by like butterflies.
More than ornamental cabbages, or orange
rays of sunset dropping their warmth on the ground,
I like to think and watch my thoughts take off like rock-

ets in a spacious place. *She* sits on her rock-
er, doing just what I do, counting seams on the trees,
conversing with bees, shaking cold coffee grounds
into the leaves. But Dame isn't the same, her cup-
id's bow lipstick awash in tears, her brow an orange
wedge of worry, and every birthday Shoo-Fly

pie comes out burned, since the night I watched her hope fly
out the window. She saw a boy atop a rock,
standing bright, steady and still as an oar angel.
He took aim and shot at a spreading tree,
knocking her popinjay from its japonica, up.
(*Please* don't tell: I saw her bird hit the ground.)

In a Picasso confusion of form and ground,
tears melted the colors and quince; her high flier
was dead, split beak and his broken body now cup-
ped in her hands. She buried him under a rock,
patting the earth with her pink Pappagallo, tre-
mendously moved by the last feather, torn orange

aflutter, as it fell on the fresh grave, arranged
with trefoil and leftover lilies. Her heel ground
a hole as she rose and spun 'round to scan the trees.
She did not spot me, only a lost lonely fly
catcher hunting for nest sites or bugs, rock to rock.

When Dame Elaine sees me nights now, I lift my cup
up to her (always alone), rocking in her cupola,
orange ground 'round the japonica tree.

Monterey Bay

Aloft, afloat, but not adrift
over dark depths,
bundled up in a sea kelp girdle,
one sunning otter recalls
the man who passed
a few days back,
pushing pools of water aside,
making his way through the bay
as though sorting the world in piles
dipping in and out of the wet record,
pausing to identify more clearly
one gull among many,
the expired pelican, folded like an envelope
as a familiar-sounding voice embraced
the crowd above
and fog obscured the distant shore
where ancient assemblies once called him
forth from dry pages to their light.

Repo Man

Great Grandpa the repo man wrote letters to his love,
long swaths of ink caught in corners of a page
mid-nightly new, from whatever rooming house
he found, his thoughts aligned for Nancy Jane
to let her know his port of call
or latest read, plots rehearsed
and standing at the ready.

Stationed west where none could track
his people down, he reclaimed vehicles
from those who failed to pay.
He took the keys; they taxied home.

He'd be the one or number three on the dance card
(he was off chasing cars, after all),
to pave the way to Baltimore and waltz his darkness
down, insert himself in reels of film
that tangled at her daddy's feet.

Once suddenly rejected,
he tore her texts, but she kept his right to the altar,
where they settled it,
never to repay that debt of love.

Ritual

In the caged-in cage
of safety, the children
bounce and freeze
and play dead man
who tags himself
back to life,
the trampoline shreds
its edges with foam
emerging and flakes
of plastic tumbling
between feet.

Holding the netting,
the frogs hop higher
squeezing their knees
to pop their young heads
above the rim
of this canister of youth:
elastic energy
released in angry nervous leaps
caught in
kid-game rules
and the need to move.

Down below in a dry field
coming reluctantly to spring,
the grown-ups gather,
circling a ceremony
for the girl's dead mother
as hawks swoop overhead
and smoke and song travel
to the loved one gone
and to the other
who jumps her rage
and never turns
her eyes away.

Louisiana Mudline

The floodwaters have abated
and a Katrina line horizontals
walls far from the musty delta.
Bodies too exhibit their mud marks,
the limits past which one goes only
to forge new territory.
So distance here moves up,
climbing windows, greasing handprints
on a stucco surface that strains
to its electrical junctures
that tie into the streetwise town
whose paving stones never drank more
than a concerted storm,
remember cartwheels,
and hold heat that speeds them dry.

Down this avenue walks a boy
who levels out his arms
the measure of a doorway
and tallies his height
against his father's.
Belted trousers hold up pants
that match now, zippered shut
and pocketed with keys.
Cuffs fall on tied shoes
that step their way
away from home,
that guide the body and its brush
to where it paints a streak
of passage black
along a fence.

Wet Exit

The man held the woman's feet
lovingly to his chest.

As he slept,
down and down she swam
into dark depths
that hid a certain light.

Her legs became a two—lane nameless road away.

Seaweed hair draped on a coral bed,
she remembered the man
only by a clutching warmth in her toes.

Miles high, the man looked down
to see he held a mermaid by the tail,
embellished with a curl of kelp.
Thinking her simply a fish,
mistaking the curve of hip
for a play of waves,
he let go—

Fishbone

The fish-spine waits,
an array of ribs hardened
to a brittle gray, in anticipation
of some cat or other
who might come along
to gnaw tenacious scent
from bending bones.
Between the vertebrae
a tendon dries,
warping the resistant palm
from its planar grip on falling flesh.
The once supple structure
stretches a spread of frozen rays,
a startled offering, his half-meshed self
like a generous sieve releasing.
What he once explored
in times more plump
could now traverse his very being.
Each carpal curve
yields less and less
to salty wave or feline tongue.

Squaring the Circling Way

No photos exist for those days,
the ones leaning into each other
as our bodies sought out spaces
where we both could be
and old lives fell away as old ways will
when the stretch into new
forms a view on the world.

For this town was our world:
a lake, a dog chasing down a piece of tree.
And we found our way finally
to the home made bed,
ringed round with glass,
the mirror, old image, paned way out.

That room became a crucible
where we distilled what would remain -
that which we've beaded out
these last four years
bright to behold and molten to the touch,
molding what will not lie still
but circles round, searching out its own tale.

Walls & Flowers

The dogwood before brick
makes her ache and bend to pat the dog at her side,
a side that cracks with tears like a roof leak
sending the message from outside
or inside
        that rips her chest away
leaving the heart to pump
like a big red tulip   pushing past ribs
like flowers through dead leaves and dirt.

Walls don't thicken swift enough
to save her
        from the expanding pressured pulse
that comes in spring
when the magnolia opens
and the smell takes her back to that heady grass rolling
still holy time.

Fur Skirt

How did she procure
that bunny-fur skirt?
Snatched it right off the rack
as my own fingers closed
on the hanger,
biting the waistband gently,
nails toothing at the belt.

Her hands were faster,
and now it feels like years.
She likely wears it
bounding swift as a snowshoe through drifts,
soft ears elongated
pink nose fighting off frost
and velvety tail
burgeoning on her backside
still hidden beneath the pale hide.

Unshaven side inward,
she jumps further when warm
and her whiskers collect
frost as snow falls.
I wish her well, after all.
Relieved of my longing
I can probe the next day's
desire for heat
and send out my hunter
to bring me back a rabbit's foot.

Frog Season

In Germany, they close the roads
to keep the cars at bay.
Lowered barriers allow
the amphibian passage
of love hops
as the road-crossing frogs
search spots to spawn.

One may have missed
my wheel this evening
as she hopped illuminated
over sodden tar
a ball of moist, delicate
skin stretched about
a web of bones:
a horizontal spark,
a spikeless star
Oh speed up!

And the spring that shot
her to the next spot
still several feet
from the gravel edge
of the courting pond
may have fallen short
of the requisite placement
respecting my wheel's
fierce chew of road,
relentless rubber
hugging wet gravel.

That last leap
might have pressed the frog's toe
or slowed her passage
between my rushing wheels
dark hulks of heaviness,
crushing orbs that kill.

Oh heighten your hop
and sing me no frog gut song.

Enlightening Jack

The last pumpkin sits
bored and tan as a lifeguard in August
waiting for nothing
but the rare thrill of catastrophe
as ants go for the corn
and worms into tomatoes.

He stays cool in his slick shell,
spread slats save him from rot
in the dark woodshed corner.

Discovered one day,
a man takes him home.
The first slit in his skull,
well, the thought makes him groan,
but the pressure relief is really a boon.
Seeds come scraping out as the light filters in,
a whole world entering through star-cut eyes.

A thought grows in his stem
as he sits on the front stoop,
spilling shaped light on the street.
He wishes to move—
some legs or a wheel or a catapult seat.
The cars swim mindless below.

So fervent his wishes,
the poor Jack starts a trembling
then a crash down the hill:
a bright gash of orange
in the new fallen snow.

Times Square Bracelet

Did the monk himself align these beads
on a stretchy string
so I might see my days arranged and circling?
Or did he gather bundles of such bracelets
to spread through the busiest
New York City intersection
while back home, his landscape lurched,
crushed, and tumbled?

The mustard robe
of little warmth slipped from his shoulders,
glowed against wet pavement's
captured light
and curled about him
like a fallen leaf, dulled
sun of the darkening afternoon wrapped
around his small form.

Tan and brown wooden balls,
some cracking after a half year
on my wrist, tell me the earth
never lies still.
We jump the fissures
and roll each day between restless fingers.

Fox

I've seen it in others,
those who smile and nod
then slip down the solitary
foxhole where wet dirt
crumbles in softly
and the dim light allows
enough to brighten a page.
Sirens wail above,
but the thick crust of earth
holds in thought vibes,
and a red-furred creature
points her snout
at a recovered line,
metes out the sounds
in a silence secured,
with a dark eye to the door.

When she's not writing in her backyard tree house, **Sarah Wyman** teaches comparative literature at the State University of New York at New Paltz. She also taught for a time at the University of Konstanz, Germany. Her scholarly work treats 20th century investigations into verbal / visual intersections, especially between poetry and painting. Recent poems have appeared in *Ekphrasis, AMP, Aaduna,* and *Mudfish*. She sharpened her pencils at Brown, Hollins, and UNC—Chapel Hill.

www.ingramcontent.com/pod-product-compliance
Lightning Source LLC
LaVergne TN
LVHW041508070426
835507LV00012B/1415